INSPIRATION

is in
HERE

Published in 2020 by Welbeck Children's Books
An Imprint of Welbeck Children's Limited, part of Welbeck Publishing Group.
20 Mortimer Street London W1T 3JW

Text & Illustrations © 2020 Welbeck Children's Limited, part of Welbeck Publishing Group.

Designed and packaged by: Duck Egg Blue Limited
Art Editor: Deborah Vickers
Editor: Jenni Lazell

ISBN 978-1-78312-646-0

Printed in Heshan, China
10 9 8 7 6 5 4 3 2 1

The publishers would like to thank the following sources for their
kind permission to reproduce the pictures in this book.
KAIT EATON: (doodles) 10–11, 15BR, 18–19
SHUTTERSTOCK: /AnaWhite: (backgrounds) 76, 110–111; /artemiya: (thumbprints) 3,
34–35; /autsawin uttisin: 68TL (background); /DigitalShards: (backgrounds) 76, 110–111;
/Ekaterina Chudakova: 60–61 (musical notes); /Flas100: 36TL (background); /Golden
Shrimp: (textures) 34TL, 58–59, 61TR, 77TL, 81TR, 86BL, 92TR; /ImHope: 82–83; /IreneArt:
20–21B (background); /Kues: (backgrounds) 7TL, 30TR, 32BL, 34TR, 41TR, 48TR, 49TR, 50BL,
51TR, 52TR, 69L, 75TL, 77, 78TL, 84TR, 86TL, 91TL, 92TL, 96–97B, 102TL, 110TL; /lena_nikolaeva:
50 (vegetables); /Leyasw: 110–111 (background); /Lu JingShan: 94TR; /Lukasz Szwaj: 53TL
(background); /m.jrn: (backgrounds) 6, 11, 32TL, 37B, 41, 46, 48, 49, 51TL, 58B, 62–63, 64TL, 69,
76TR, 84C, 89, 94–95B, 99, 110TL, 112; /Ohn Mar: 89TR; /Olga Pasynkova: 32–33 (background);
/Paladin12: 108–109 (background); /Polina Tomtosova: 89TC; /Pupsikland: (backgrounds)
27L, 77BR, 106, 107; /Pyty: 95 (morse code); /Sk_Advance studio: (backgrounds) 3, 4–5,
10–11, 64–65, 74T; /StockAppeal: 52–53B (background); /stockninja: 97TR (cross-hatches); /
Strawberry Blossom: (backgrounds) 41, 52; /Svekas: 48–49 (background); /Ton Weerayut
Photographer: (backgrounds) 96TL, 97T; /tuulijumala: 65TR; /Uspenskaya A: 89L; /
VolodymyrSanych: (backgrounds) 6–7, 30, 32–33B, 70–71B, 75, 90–91, 94BL; /xenia_ok:
64–65 (zodiac signs)
Every effort has been made to acknowledge correctly and contact
the source and/or copyright holder of each picture any unintentional
errors or omissions will be corrected in future editions of this book.

INSPIRATION

is in
HERE

WELBECK

Written by Laura Baker

Illustrated by Tjarda Borsboom

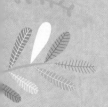

Contents

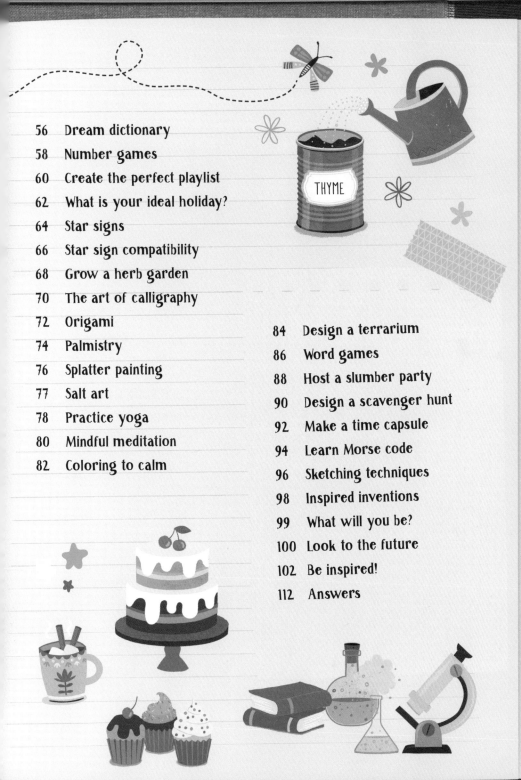

Seeking inspiration?

If you're looking for a little inspiration in your life, you've come to the right place!

What is inspiration?

Inspiration is all about finding the encouragement and imagination to do something. It can sneak up in quiet moments or burst in, big and bright. It can come from others, or it can grow from within. Inspiration is what you make of it.

By learning from others

From your own challenges and successes

In stories

Where can you find it?

In this book!

By looking closely at nature

From people who do things that you admire — big or small

By taking a moment to breathe and listen

In art

What's inside?

Within these pages, you'll find inspiration to train your brain, encouragement to dream and set goals, ideas for drawing, support for learning new skills, and so much more. Dive into the pages that call you, or work through them one by one. Just follow your heart, and inspiration won't be far behind!

Inspiration is closer than you think.

What does inspiration mean to you?

Things that inspire me

....
....
....
....
....

How I feel when I'm inspired

....
....
....
....
....
....
....
....

People who inspire me

....
....
....
....
....
....
....

All about you

This space is just waiting to be filled with your hopes, goals, and dreams.

This year, I hope to:

1 _____

2 _____

3 _____

In five years, I will be ____ years old.
I hope to be:

1 _____

2 _____

3 _____

I dream that:

1 _____

2 _____

3 _____

Sometimes I worry that:

1 _____

2 _____

3 _____

Inspiration here!

Your fears are just as important as your hopes and dreams. Writing them down helps you acknowledge and work through them, all the way to success.

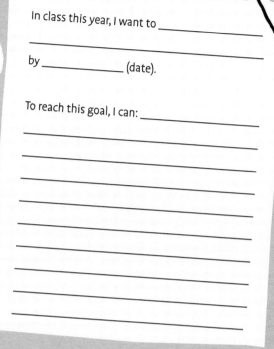

Be real

A goal should be a dream that you can actually achieve. Make sure that it is realistic, with a set outcome and deadline.

In class this year, I want to _____ _____
by _____ (date).

To reach this goal, I can: _____ _____ _____ _____ _____ _____ _____ _____ _____ _____ _____

At home this year, I want to _____ _____
by _____ (date).

To reach this goal, I can: _____ _____ _____ _____ _____ _____ _____ _____ _____ _____ _____

Shape challenge

Warm up your creativity with this delightful doodling exercise.

What do you see in this shape?

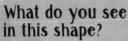

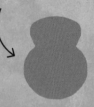

A monster?

A bird?

A yummy treat!

How about this one?

A fish?

A face?

A spaceship!

Take on the challenge

Add your own doodles to bring these shapes to life.

Pass on the challenge

Create your own doodling challenge. Draw some random shapes, and see how they inspire your friends.

How to draw cute animals

Unicorn

1 With a pencil, draw a small circle and a bigger one next to it.

2 Connect the circles as shown. Draw a nostril, snout line, eye, and ear.

3 Draw the mane in swooping lines, as shown.

4 Add a horn and more detail to the mane and ear.

5 Draw an L-shaped line down from the head and over to the bottom of the mane for a neck.

6 Erase any inner pencil lines, then color your mystical wonder!

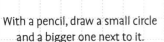

Sloth

1 Use your pencil to draw a heart shape with a rounded bottom. Draw a bean shape around this.

2 Add big eyes, a triangle nose, and a smile.

3 Draw a curved arm and leg, both reaching above the sloth.

4 Add a tummy line and long, pointed claws to the arm and leg. Erase any inner pencil lines.

5 Lightly sketch lots of short lines on the body for fur and draw a branch for the sloth to hold on to.

6 Draw another arm and leg reaching up from behind the sloth. Add color to your cute creature.

Write a superhero story

Follow this formula to write an exhilarating superhero story full of ups, downs, and adventures.

Story structure

All stories need a beginning, an end, and some things that happen in between. A common structure divides the story into three acts.

ACT 1
DEPARTURE FROM ORDINARY LIFE

★ Show us where the hero of your story lives and what he or she is like normally. Are they shy or outgoing? Where do they live?

★ Then, adventure calls! This could be something big like an earthquake or small like a phone call. Either way, it disrupts the comfort of the ordinary world and sets up a challenge for the hero.

The hero might speak to someone who gives them a gift or advice to help them on their way.

ACT 2
INTO THE UNKNOWN

Along the way the hero meets friends who help and enemies who hinder.

★ The hero begins their quest and is faced with a series of challenges. Maybe the villain throws different tests at them as they approach. Huge robots? A sinking ship?

★ Finally, the hero reaches their biggest challenge—this is usually the villain in a superhero story. If the hero doesn't succeed, they could lose everything.

★ The hero defeats the enemy and comes out a stronger person than they were before.

ACT 3
A HERO'S RETURN

★ The hero finds their way back home and might have smaller challenges to face as they go.

★ They must now come to terms with the changed person they have become and find a way to live in the new world they have created.

Build a world

Think about the world where your story takes place. What does it look like? What sounds can you hear? What smells can you pick up? Make sure to describe these throughout your story.

Word magic

Language is a powerful tool to create the feel of your story. Try to include some superhero words like these:

AMAZING   RESPONSIBILITY   POW

POWERFUL   SECRET   WHAM
                  IDENTITY

              HERO

SAVE THE DAY!   COURAGE   EVIL   DOOM

      HELP!

VILLAIN   INVINCIBLE   BOOM   INCREDIBLE

Gaze at the stars

Look up, and you'll discover a whole sky full of stories and wonder.

For the perfect night of stargazing, you will need:

★ a warm coat (if it's cold outside)
★ blankets to lie on
★ a friend or grownup to join you
★ a clear sky without clouds
★ a garden away from city lights

Stories in the sky

From the earliest days of stargazing, thousands of years ago, people have been looking for patterns in the stars. These are called constellations, and are named after mythical heroes, animals, or objects that astronomers saw in the stars. Ancient Greek stargazers named 48 constellations. Today, scientists recognise 88.

Make a wish

Shooting stars aren't stars at all, but meteors. They are space debris burning up as they reach Earth's atmosphere. Watch the sky carefully and make a wish as you see one go by!

BIG DIPPER
part of
Ursa Major

URSA MAJOR
the great bear

THE NORTH STAR

URSA MINOR
the smaller bear

A matter of time

As Earth spins through space, the stars we see change. The night sky looks different depending on the time of year, and whether you are in the Northern or Southern Hemisphere of the planet.

DRACO
the dragon

NORTHERN CROSS
part of Cygnus

CYGNUS
the swan

CONSTELLATION KEY

——— NORTHERN HEMISPHERE

——— SOUTHERN HEMISPHERE

CENTAURUS
the centaur
(half human, half horse)

CARINA
the keel of a ship

SOUTHERN CROSS

Be an astronomer

Take a notebook with you as you stare at the skies. Sketch what you see, and make up your own names for the patterns.

Inspiration here!

There are more stars in the universe than there are grains of sand on all the beaches of Earth combined.

Make bath bombs

Follow these steps to make fun bathtime accessories to fizz your worries away.

You will need:

★ 1 cup baking soda
★ ½ cup citric acid powder
★ ¼ cup cornstarch
★ 2 tbsp warmed coconut oil
★ liquid food coloring (whatever color you want your bath bombs to be)
★ water
★ bath bomb molds (see note opposite)

NOTE: ⚠️
Always wash your hands after handling citric acid.

TIP
You can buy citric acid powder online or from drugstores.

1

Measure the baking soda, citric acid, and cornstarch into a large mixing bowl. Whisk together until combined.

2

coconut oil

In a separate bowl, mix together the coconut oil and a few drops of food coloring.

3

Add the liquid mixture to the dry ingredients a little bit at a time, whisking after every addition. When you've poured in all the oil mixture, add a few drops of water and mix in quickly. You want the mixture to hold when pressed together but not be too wet.

4

Pack your mixture tightly into molds. Leave to set in a cool, dry place overnight.

Inspiration here!

You can buy bath bomb molds at craft shops, or you can find your own around the house. Try muffin pans, rinsed-out yogurt pots or silicone ice cube trays.

5

Very carefully, taking your time, remove the bath bombs from the molds. Then drop in the bath when you're ready to relax!

These bath bombs are for fun, fizzing purposes only. Never eat them!

Feel the fizz

The fizz of a bath bomb comes from the baking soda reacting with the citric acid in water. Science suds!

Keep a personalized planner

Personalized planners bring
reflection and calm to busy life plans.

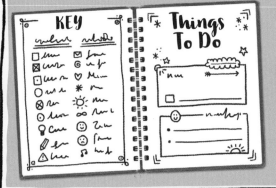

What is a personalized planner?

This smart system combines journaling with calendar diaries. It's a place to record things to do, including space for goals and reflections. Most importantly, it is perfectly tailored to you.

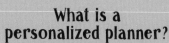
You might want to use a notebook with a pretty cover, or you could decorate your own to make it just your style.

1

Where do I start?
Find a blank notebook. The pages can be lined or plain—it's up to you!

2

Clever key
Come up with a system that works for you, and write this down on the first page of your planner.

+×+×+×+×+×+× KEY ×+×+×+×+×+×+

☐ To do   💡 Idea
✓ Done!   ◎ Inspirational note
○ Event   ✳ Top priority

Add doodles to show the weather each day, or to represent something special that happened.

3

Set it up

Draw a box for each day of the week on the lefthand page. On the righthand page, draw boxes for things you'd like to record that week. This could include books you read, movies you watched, or funny moments.

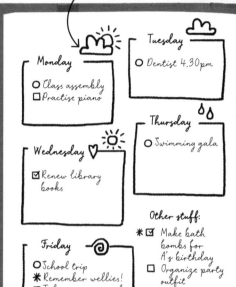

Monday
- ○ Class assembly
- ☐ Practise piano

Tuesday
- ○ Dentist 4.30pm

Wednesday
- ☑ Renew library books

Thursday
- ○ Swimming gala

Friday
- ○ School trip
- ✳ Remember wellies!
- ☐ Tidy my room, urgh

Other stuff:
- ✳ ☑ Make bath bombs for A's birthday
- ☐ Organize party outfit
- ○ Sat 3pm - football match!

Quote of the week: Make **TODAY** count!

Happy times: ☺

Best books:

× + × + × + × + × + × + × + × + × + × + × + × + × + × + × + × + × +

Notes
- ○ Ada's party next Tuesday!
- ○ Fundraising ideas
    - cake sale?
    - disco?

My mood this week:

4

Fill it in

Then, as the week goes on, fill up the page. Write down tasks, events, and notes each day, and record plans, memories and highlights in the boxes on the right. Do the same for the next week, and the next.

You might also want to include a page with space for monthly plans and reflections, and one looking ahead to the year.

You do you

You might love to draw, or have great handwriting. Decorate the pages in your own special style. Create gorgeous pictures and swirly letters, or write down every little thing. Do what feels right to you.

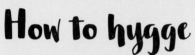

How to hygge

"Hygge" is the Danish word for cozy comfort that brings contentment and happiness—and it's taking over the world!

sweet smelling candles

That Hygge feeling

Hygge is said to be a part of the Danish lifestyle. People smile, nod at each other, and feel a sense of contentment. The Danish people are often called the happiest in the world. What can we do to feel this happiness too?

wooly socks

fresh plants

relaxed setting

How else can you find this happy inner peace?

Exercise

A chat with friends

Spending time with a pet

good book

cozy blanket

Inspiration here!

In 2016, the word "hygge" was so popular that it was a finalist for the Oxford Dictionaries' word of the year. "Hygge" is pronounced "hoo-guh."

hot chocolate on a cold day

freshly baked cookies

Meditation

Doing something kind for a stranger

Noticing the little things

Write a haiku

Challenge yourself to write about a moment in nature using this poetic pattern.

What is a haiku?

A haiku is a Japanese poem that uses a set number of syllables per line to describe nature and the seasons. These poems were first written over 400 years ago.

The pattern

The poem is divided into three lines:

5 syllables

7 syllables

5 syllables

Syllables are like beats. Clap as you say each one to help you count them.

① ② ③   ① ② ③ ④
sy / lla / ble   clap / as / you / go

Take a look at these tiny masterpieces:

① ② ③ ④ ⑤
An old silent pond . . .
① ② ③ ④ ⑤ ⑥ ⑦
A frog jumps into the pond,
① ② ③ ④ ⑤
splash! Silence again.

by Matsuo Basho

Light candy-floss clouds.
Sunshine and laughter abound—
Perfect summer's day.

There is often a pause at the end of the second line, before the last line sums up the poem.

twinkle   sunset   crisp   warm   rustling leaves

A world in words

moon

In this short poem, you have only a few words to use, so think carefully about the ones you choose. Make use of language that conveys the feel of the moment or season you're describing.

cool

sun

breeze   snow   blossoming
blanket   starry

Write an acrostic poem

An acrostic poem is unique in that it reads down the page as well as across.

C H K R G Z E T P W O B S M N Y U

What is an acrostic poem?

An acrostic poem is made of words formed from the letters of a main word that is the theme of the poem.

How do I write one?

Choose your main word and write this down the page. Then write a line beginning with each letter of the main word. Finish this poem with your own ideas on what makes you happy.

Hugs
A
P
P
Y

In the glow of the setting sun,
Not a sound from anyone,
Secrets whisper in my ear,
Powerful ideas I can hear,
Inspiring me to do and see,
Raising me up to go set free
Everything that I can be.

Fun
Reliable
g**I**ggles
Endless chats
Nobody better
Don't come between us!

NOTE:
Each line could be simply a word that describes your theme, or a longer phrase.

TIP
If you're struggling to find a phrase that starts with a letter in your main word, use that letter in the middle of a line instead.

Go create!

Write your own acrostic poem. You could describe a friend, writing their name down the page, or how about your favourite holiday?

Unearth your family tree

Delve into your past to discover your family's stories and fill in your family tree.

What is genealogy?

Genealogy is the study of ancestry: tracing your family back through generations. It can include how people are connected, where families come from and what their ancestors did way back in the past. A family tree shows the relationships amongst people in one line of ancestry.

Dig deep

You may not have all the names and dates to fill in your family tree straight away. Try these tips to get to the roots of what you're looking for:

- Speak to relatives. They can often help fill in a lot of gaps.

- Look at old newspaper clippings, birth certificates, letters, and photo albums for names, dates, and connections.

- Check local family history societies and national archives.

- Search online genealogy websites, but be aware that some charge fees.

Fill in the name and date of birth for each entry.

Collect stories

While you're speaking to family, ask them to tell you stories they remember of their relatives . . . anything from their past! Collect these special memories by writing them down in a family history journal for future generations to discover.

Great-grandparents

Grandparents

Parents

Me and my siblings

Inspiration here!

One of the longest and fullest family trees ever recorded is of Chinese philosopher Confucius. The tree covers 2,500 years, over 80 generations and more than two million descendants.

What's your spirit animal?

Take this quiz to unveil your secret spirit animal.

WARNING: MAY RESULT IN SELF-DISCOVERY!

What is a spirit animal?

A spirit animal is not only an animal you identify with, but one that sees the world in the way you do and can guide you through life. Spirit animals appear in many different cultures in many different forms.

1 At a party, you can find me...

A. Fluttering around the room talking to everybody there.
B. Smiling and laughing with friends.
C. Taking shy friends under my wing.
D. Watching everyone closely from the corner.

2 My must have item for a holiday is...

A. My favorite pair of sunglasses.
B. My teddy.
C. A journal.
D. A map.

3 My favorite element is...

A. Air.
B. Water.
C. Earth.
D. Fire.

4 My dream job is...

A. I don't know yet! I'll try lots to find out.
B. An artist.
C. A teacher.
D. President.

5 On the weekend, I love to...

A. Try something new every week.
B. Peacefully promote my favorite cause.
C. Hang out with friends.
D. Go to the library.

6 I'm moving to a new school. I feel . . .

A. Excited! I can't wait to make new friends.
B. Hopeful. I will find joy in this change.
C. Brave. I'm a little nervous but I can do this.
D. Fine. I'll focus on my work and I'll be all right.

7 Most important in a friend is . . .

A. Someone I can laugh with.
B. Someone I get along with.
C. Someone who needs me.
D. Someone who will challenge me.

Mostly As
You're a
BUTTERFLY

Fly free, sweet butterfly! You live life lightly and flutter towards joy. You are not afraid of change and see it as a chance for growth and rebirth. You will go through life and the transformations it brings with grace in your soul.

Mostly Bs
You're a
DOLPHIN

Though you may be gentle on the outside, you have inner strength. You strive for peace and harmony and have found a balance between intelligence and intuition. You are a friend to everyone. Your playful, joyful attitude will take you far.

Mostly Cs
You're a
BEAR

Strong, confident, and brave, you are a born leader. Though you like time alone, you will always be the first to help others. You will use your strength to protect and guide your friends.

Mostly Ds
You're a
WOLF

Just like a wolf, you're sharp and smart. You have incredible instinct and follow it boldly. You may sometimes have trust issues that cause you fear, but follow your instincts, and you will live freely.

Make an inspiration jar

Create your own inspiration with this jar of encouragement that you can reach into whenever you need it.

You will need:
★ a large glass jar
★ colored paper
★ string, ribbon, or any other items for decoration

1

Carefully clean out your jar. Leave to dry.

2

Decorate the jar. You might want to stick on colored paper stars, give the jar a pretty label, or tie string or ribbon around the neck.

3

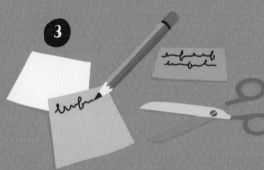

Write inspiring messages on the colored paper. Cut out each message and place in the jar. Close the lid.

4

Reach into the jar any time you need inspiration!

TIP
Copy some of the inspirational messages on the opposite page, or be inspired to write your own!

It's not that I'm so smart, it's just that I stay with problems longer.
– Einstein

Mistakes pave the path to success.

You are the only YOU.

Just breathe.

Believe you can and you're halfway there. – Theodore Roosevelt

Smile at everyone today. You never know who needs it.

Never stop trying.

Dream big.

Kindness counts.

I have learned you are never too small to make a difference.
– Greta Thunberg

Dream big

Your jar doesn't have to hold only inspiration.
Try these ideas, or come up with others.

Confidence jar

Write down your successes
—big or small—to remind
yourself how strong you are
whenever you need a boost
of confidence.

Smile jar

Fill the jar with notes
and pictures that make
you smile. Take one out
each time you need to
brighten your day.

Hopes and dreams

Note your hopes for the future and your dreams for yourself,
your family and friends. Every so often, dive into the jar to pull
out one note. This could act as a reminder of your hopes or a
nudge to start working towards the dream.

Learn to crochet

Develop patience and creativity as you take up this clever handicraft.

What is crochet?

Crochet uses a hooked needle and a series of stitches and woven knots to turn wool into beautiful textured patterns.

The slip knot

1 Hold the wool between your left thumb and middle finger, draping about 15 cm over the index finger as shown. The end of the yarn should be in the front.

2 Using your right hand, hold the hook like a pencil, facing up. Slide it between the wool and your index finger.

3 Use the hook to lift the wool up. Twist the hook in a circle to create a twisted loop of wool.

4 Hold the loose end of wool between your left thumb and middle finger and use your index finger to guide the wool unwinding from the ball. Wrap the wool over your left index finger from behind and tuck it under the hook, as shown.

5 Use the hook to pull the wool through the loop you made earlier. Pull gently on the ends of the wool to tighten the slip knot on the hook. Be sure you can still move the hook freely.

6 You should now have a knot on your hook. You have started crocheting!

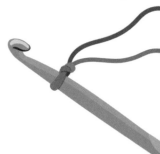

The single chain

Create a slip knot.

2

Using your left hand, bring the long end of wool from the back to the front of the hook, and hook it.

3

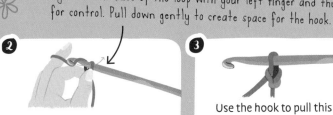

Use the hook to pull this wool through the slip knot loop, leaving it on the hook. This is your first chain stitch.

Again, bring the long end of wool from the back to the front of the hook and hook it.

5

Pull this through the new loop. This is your next chain stitch.

6

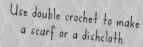

Repeat until the chain is as long as you like!

Double crochet

This technique is used in most crochet patterns.
Master it and you'll open up a world of crochet options!

Use double crochet to make a scarf or a dishcloth.

...art with the hook facing up. Twist it down to help guide ...t through loops, then up again to view the loop created.

1

Create a chain as described above.

2

Now look carefully at your chain. It should be formed from a series of V shapes. Count two Vs back from your hook. Poke your hook through the left part of the second V, as shown.

3

As before, bring the long end of the wool from the back to the front of the hook and hook it. Pull this wool through the V shape only and twist your hook upwards. You should now have two loops on the hook.

4

Again, bring the long end of the wool from the back to the front of the hook and hook it. Pull this wool through both loops so you end up with one loop on the hook and two below. This is your first double crochet stitch.

5

Repeat steps 2 to 4 in the next V in the chain, and the next, until you reach the end of the chain. Then go back the other way, working into this new row.

Design a den

Create a cozy indoor hideaway where you can read, write, draw, or chill with friends.

Perfect spot

Where will you build your indoor den? You could use a clear space in your living room or bedroom, or find a cozy nook such as a window seat or large fitted wardrobe.

Pile cushions and blankets on the floor for cozy comfort.

Cardboard creations

Instead of using blankets and chairs, try building a den made of big cardboard boxes and craft tape. Use felt-tip pens and paints to decorate.

Place chairs facing outwards around the edge of where you want your den to be.

Drape sheets and blankets over the chairs to create a canopy. Use clothes pegs to secure them in place.

Safely string fairy lights around your den for an enchanted feel.

WARNING!
Never light candles in an indoor den. If you'd like that magical look, try battery-operated candles instead.

Think theme
You could choose a theme and decorate your den to fit. Are you a movie fan? Put movie posters and Hollywood stars up everywhere! Do you love stories? Fill your library den with books.

Keep books, paper, pens, and pencils in your den ready for when inspiration strikes.

Fingerprint doodles

Bring your fingerprints to life with cute, crazy and creative doodles.

You will need:

★ washable ink pads or paint
★ felt-tip pens
★ paper or card

NOTE:
If you're using paint, pour a small amount on to a plate.

Fingerprint family

Use different fingers and your thumb to make doodles of varying sizes. You can even create a whole family of doodle prints!

1 Press your finger or thumb on to the ink or paint.

2 Press your finger or thumb on to paper or card to make a print. Let dry. Wipe the ink or paint off your hand.

Clever combos

Put prints together to make more complex characters and scenes.

3 Doodle away!

Handing it over to you

Draw on these prints, then add your own fingerprints to cover in doodles.

Cute or quirky? You decide!

The language of flowers

Learn the language of flowers and use beautiful blooms for your own meaningful keepsakes.

Forget-me-not
memories of true love

Feelings in floral

Flowers have a language of their own: each one has been given its own meaning. You can tell someone how you feel by the flower you choose to give them.

Red rose
love

Daisy
hope, innocence

Bluebell
kindness, humility

Pink carnation
I'll never forget you

Pink rose
happiness

Calla lily
beauty

Willow
sadness

NOTE:
Never pick flowers from someone's garden. Ask an adult if you can take a flower from your own garden or buy some from a florist.

Press flowers

Press flowers to preserve their beauty.

You will need:
- ★ freshly-picked flowers
- ★ a heavy book
- ★ baking paper

1

Gather clean, dry flowers on a sunny day. Remove the stems.

2

Find a thick, heavy book and open it towards the end. Lay a piece of baking paper on the righthand page. Place your flowers on the paper.

3

Lay another piece of baking paper on top of the flowers. Then close the book.

4

Use tweezers to lift the flowers carefully.

Leave for a week or more. Check that the flowers are fully dried out and papery before carefully removing.

Pressed flower phone case

Use your pressed flowers for a fantastically whimsical phone case.

You will need:
- ★ a plain phone case
- ★ pressed flowers
- ★ clear nail varnish or resin

1 Get hold of a simple, plain phone case.

2 Arrange your flowers on the case. You could use tiny dabs of glue, clear nail varnish, or resin to keep the flowers in place.

3 Paint clear nail varnish or resin over the flowers and the whole of the case. Leave to dry completely.

Start a secret journal

Fill a notebook with memories, thoughts, and feelings for your eyes only.

What is a journal?

A journal is a private place for you to write all about you. You might want to record what happens every day: who you saw, what you did, and highlights you never want to forget.

How?

The best thing about journals is ... there are no rules! This is your space, so use it how you like. Write everything in neat lines, or scribble all over the page. Draw what you see instead of using words. Add stickers or photos, and use your nicest pens. It's up to you!

Where?

Find a cozy, quiet spot where you can reflect, write, and lose yourself in your thoughts.

Free writing

If you're stuck on what to say, try free writing. Just write what comes to mind, without worrying where it's going.

The journal is your friend

Sometimes writing down problems and worries can help you work through them. Talk to your journal like a friend. It's a safe and welcoming space.

Give it a go

Practise journaling here. Try free writing about your day, and see where it takes you!

The art of letter writing

Some say that letter writing is a lost art,
but you can find a love for it again.

Why send a letter?

Letters are handwritten, making them personal and meaningful. Instead of typing a quick text, you're spending the time to write to someone. That makes them feel special and important.

When would you send a letter?

Letters can be for special occasions or just because. People often send them to say:

thank you for a gift

I'm sorry

I love you

hello to someone far away

What should you write?

October 22nd, 2020 ← date

Dear Jessica,

Thank you so much for the beautiful notebook you gave me for my birthday. I use it as a diary, to capture all my thoughts, ideas, and special things I have done each day.

Love Molly x

↑ sign your name

your message: tell the reader something specific about their gift or your life at the moment

Inspiration here!

You can save your letters as treasured keepsakes. The date helps place the memories.

Treat yourself

Letter writing can be luxurious. Find beautiful stationery, fancy pens, and even a seal for the envelope to make your letters extra special.

Cutout cards

Create a clever peep through card to send a friend.

You will need:

★ an A4 piece of card
★ fabric or tissue paper
★ felt-tip pens

1

Fold a piece of card in half lengthwise. Cut along this line.

2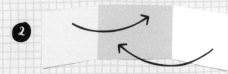

Take one strip of card and hold it with the short ends on the sides. Fold in each end towards the center so that they overlap equally, as shown. Press down.

3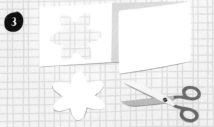

Ask an adult to help you carefully cut out a shape in the left flap.

4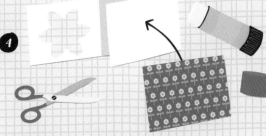

Lay your fabric or tissue paper over the right flap and cut it to size. Glue this on the right flap and leave to dry. Remember that you'll see it through the cut out shape.

5

Fold the left flap over the right flap to create your card. Decorate the front, and write your message inside.

Inspiration here!

What is your card for? If it's a birthday card, you could cut out a balloon or cake shape. If it's for Christmas, try a Christmas tree!

Motivating mind games

Keep your brain in shape with these stimulating memory games and puzzles.

Riddle me this

A riddle is a puzzle of words.
Can you solve these puzzling questions?

What has a neck but no head?

What is so delicate that saying its name breaks it?

I'm tall when I'm young and short when I'm old.

What am I?

Memory magic

Set a timer and study this picture for 30 seconds. Now cover it with a piece of paper.

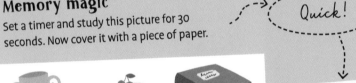

Quick!

How many items can you remember from the image? List them here.

Shopping list

Gather a group of friends to play this memory game.

The first person thinks of an item beginning with A. Then they say, for example . . .

I went shopping and I bought an avocado.

The next person repeats the sentence and adds an item beginning with B. They say, for example . . .

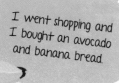

I went shopping and I bought an avocado and banana bread.

The game goes on like this, adding an item for each letter of the alphabet.

How far can you get before someone forgets?

I went shopping and I bought, uh . . .

What's missing?

Look carefully at this picture for 30 seconds. Now cover it with a piece of paper.

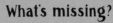

Now look at the picture below. Which two objects are in this picture that weren't in the first one?

An interview with you

The spotlight is on you! Imagine a magazine journalist wants to interview you for a special feature. What would you say?

Draw or cut and stick a profile picture of you here.

What did you have for breakfast today?
....
....

What is your favorite book?
....
....

If you could have any superpower, what would you choose and why?
....
....
....
....
....
....

What are you most excited about?
....
....
....

What is your favorite class in school?
....
....

What does a normal day look like for you?
....
....
....
....
....
....

Where would you love to visit?
....
....

Do you prefer...

Circle your answer.

sweet or savory?

cats or dogs?

day or night?

beach or mountain?

summer or winter?

scary movies or happy endings?

calls or texts?

bath or shower?

sneakers or sandals?

cinema or movie at home?

save or spend?

hoodie or sweater?

eat in or takeaway?

city or countryside?

bowling or skating?

What makes you happy?

....
....
....
....
....
....
....
....
....

If you could be any type of food, what would you be and why?

....
....
....
....
....
....
....

45

Are you an introvert or an extrovert?

Take this quiz to discover the best way for you to recharge.

Psychology speak
Introversion and extroversion are terms used by psychologists to describe how people are motivated and where they get their energy.

Tick each answer that applies to you:

☐ I love to invite the whole class to my birthday parties, instead of just a few friends.

☐ After a busy weekend, I can't wait to catch up with my friends in class.

☐ I often interrupt people when they talk. I get so excited to join in!

☐ At a party, I am always dancing in the middle of the dance floor.

☐ I would love to be a famous singer or actor one day.

☐ I could talk on the phone for hours!

☐ I love working on group projects and sharing my ideas as we go along.

☐ I am comfortable in new places.

☐ I leave parties and activities feeling excited, even if they were tiring.

☐ I flit from friend to friend, happy to talk to whoever is around.

☐ If my friends are arguing, I get in the middle to help them out.

☐ I talk more than I listen.

☐ I sometimes start projects that I forget to finish.

☐ I get grumpy if I'm stuck inside for too long.

☐ Rollercoasters are the best!

The results are in . . .

Count the number of ticks that you marked on the opposite page. Now read your result below.

0-5 ticks

You're an *introvert!*

You are calm, considered, and enjoy spending time on your own. You prefer small groups to big parties and can become overwhelmed or drained in large social situations. You recharge best with some time alone. Grab a cozy blanket and a good book or movie, and settle in for a quiet night!

Climate activist Greta Thunberg identifies as an introvert. She focuses on her thoughts, which help her to see things in new ways. She believes that one introvert can change the world.

6-10 ticks

You're a *mix* of both!

Sometimes you like to be alone, and other times you're drawn to hanging out with your friends. Your emotions guide you, but you can be swayed by other people's opinions, too. Pay close attention to what gives you energy and find just the right balance for you.

Hello!

A well-known extrovert is innovator Steve Jobs. His ability to deliver engaging speeches and motivate his team turned his ideas into realities.

11-15 ticks

You're an *extrovert!*

You're outgoing, enthusiastic, and you love to be surrounded by people. You work well in groups and can become bored when on your own. You find energy from social settings. Gather a group of friends and get chatting!

Making prints

Find objects around the house to bring new life to your paintings.

You will need:
- ★ potatoes
- ★ cookie cutters
- ★ paint and paintbrush
- ★ paper

Potato prints

1 Ask an adult to cut a potato in half.

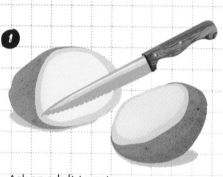

2 Press a cookie cutter firmly into one half of the potato, as far as you can.

Cut down a small amount so that your stamp is raised.

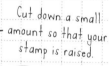

3 Ask an adult to cut around the cookie cutter with a small knife. Peel away the excess potato, then remove the cookie cutter.

4 Use a paintbrush to cover your stamp in a thin layer of paint. Then press the stamp down on your page!

Pointillism practice

Use a pencil eraser to try this famous painting technique.

Cut out a colorful picture from a magazine.

You will need:
★ a picture from a magazine
★ paint
★ an old pencil with an eraser on the end

Dip your pencil eraser in colored paint. Dab dots on the picture, matching your paint color to the colored sections on the page.

Then try creating your own pointillism painting, without the background picture.

Widen your search
Be inspired to look for other different sized objects for stamping. You could try:

recycled foam packaging

cotton swabs

bubble wrap

corks

vegetables

leaves

Inspiration here!

Pointillism was developed by artists Georges Seurat and Paul Signac in 1886. It uses loads of small dots to make up a bigger picture.

Start cooking

Cooking covers many techniques, tastes, and methods. Learn some of the basics and get inspired to get started!

Stay safe

Ask an adult to help with knives, ovens, and raw meat.

Always wash your hands before cooking, as well as after handling raw meat and eggs.

Use separate cutting boards for meat, veg, fish, and bread.

Ingredients

As much as you can, use fresh ingredients. Shop from your local fruit and veg shop, and grow vegetables and herbs in your garden if possible.

Food science

Get to know what different ingredients do in a dish. For example, adding something acidic, such as lemon juice, balances out sweet and salty flavors.

Different diets

People choose to eat only some foods and cut out others for various reasons.

Vegetarian
Does not eat meat or fish

Pescatarian
Does not eat meat; eats fish

Vegan
Does not eat meat, fish, dairy, or eggs

Flexitarian
Mostly vegetarian, but sometimes eats meat and fish

Seasoning

Seasonings are essential to any cook's kitchen. They include salt, pepper, herbs, and other spices. Get to know them and try them in your dishes. Always test and taste as you go, to get just the perfect flavor at the end.

Personal pizzas

Make your very own personalized pizza following these simple steps.

You will need:

* ★ a mini pitta or naan bread
* ★ tomato puree
* ★ chopped toppings of your choice
* ★ mozzarella cheese

Always ask an adult to help with using the oven.

1 Preheat the oven to 350° F. Place the pitta or naan on a baking tray. Spread tomato puree on the pitta or naan.

2 Cut the mozzarella cheese into small cubes, or grate it carefully. Sprinkle your cheese and toppings generously over your pizza.

3 Ask an adult to put the tray in the oven. Bake for 4-5 minutes, until the cheese is a lovely golden brown.

TIP

Sprinkling your toppings from a height (holding your hand high above the pizza) helps them fall evenly around the bread, rather than in clumps.

Pizza party!

Have a pizza party with your friends. Let each person decorate their own personal pizza with toppings of their choice. Then cook!

Toppings galore

Your pizza toppings could include:

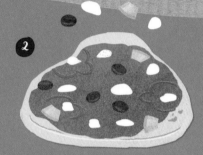

olives

onion

peppers

tomatoes

mushrooms

sweetcorn

pineapple

Sweet fruit kebabs

Create a gorgeous treat that is impressive to look at, delicious to eat—and easy to make!

You will need:
★ fresh fruit (such as strawberries, blueberries, banana, apple, and kiwi)
★ 3.5 oz plain chocolate
★ long wooden skewers

Vegetarian-friendly recipe! Dairy-free chocolate makes this vegan-friendly.

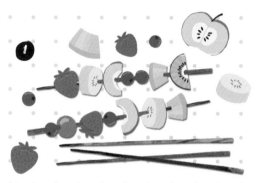

Chop your fruit into bite-sized pieces. Carefully push several pieces on to each skewer. Try making a pattern, such as strawberry, blueberry, banana, strawberry, blueberry, banana.

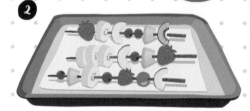

Line a baking sheet with baking paper. Lay the fruit kebabs flat on this sheet.

Break the plain chocolate into a microwave-safe bowl. Microwave on medium power for 1 minute. Stir. Microwave for another minute. Stir until smooth.

Use a spoon to drizzle the chocolate over your kebabs.

Mix it up
For added wow factor, try melting white chocolate as well as plain. Drizzle both over the fruit for a cool look. You could even dust sprinkles over the top for a party pop.

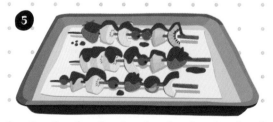

Leave in the fridge for an hour to set.

The beauty of baking

The act of baking can be truly relaxing, while the results can be positively scrumptious!

Tools

Gather these tools of the trade for all your baking adventures:

- weighing scale
- mixing bowls
- baking trays
- whisk
- wooden spoon
- measuring spoons

Did you know?

Technically, cooking means any mixing and heating to create a dish. Baking is a type of cooking. It uses a heat that doesn't touch the food directly, such as in an oven. Cooking is said to be an **art**, while baking is a precise **science**.

Top tips

Cook like a pro with these bakers' secrets.

Read a recipe all the way through before starting. That way you'll be sure you have all the ingredients, tools, and timings right.

To beat eggs, use a fork and hold it flat on the eggs. Whisk with your wrist.

Practice, practice, practice! Test different bakes and try new things.

Don't swap baking powder for baking soda. Baking soda reacts with an acid and a liquid to help baked goods rise. Baking powder contains its own acid and needs only a liquid to be activated.

When measuring liquid ingredients, bend down so your eyes are level with the markings on the measuring cup.

53

Start a dream diary

Keep a journal to remember the stories that come to you in the night.

Catching dreams

Dreams are funny, flitting things. They can be so vivid in your sleep, still clear when you wake up, but gone when you try to remember them later in the day. Catch their memories by writing them down in a diary when you first wake. Try to capture what happened.

See if you can remember what your dream looked like, who was there, and even any smells or sounds you could pick up.

DIARY

Keep your notebook on your bedside table so that you can write down your dream while it's still fresh in your mind.

Dreamy details

In your diary, you could also note down:

★ if you've had the dream before

★ how real it felt

★ if it affected your sleep

★ any patterns you can spot in the dreams in your diary

Inspiration here!

Psychologist Carl Jung studied dreams. He suggested that a series of your dreams over time could tell a hidden story of your life.

54

My dream diary

Try keeping a dream diary here for a few days to get started.

On Monday I dreamed about _____
_____
_____
_____

I felt _____
I've had this dream before: Yes ☐   No ☐

On Tuesday I dreamed about _____
_____
_____
_____

I felt _____
I've had this dream before: Yes ☐   No ☐

On Wednesday I dreamed about _____
_____
_____
_____

I felt _____
I've had this dream before: Yes ☐   No ☐

On Thursday I dreamed about _____
_____
_____
_____

I felt _____
I've had this dream before: Yes ☐   No ☐

On Friday I dreamed about _____
_____
_____
_____

I felt _____
I've had this dream before: Yes ☐   No ☐

Dream dictionary

Discover the meanings of your dreams
with this dream dictionary.

The language of dreams

Dream psychologists believe
that dreams can come
from your imagination
and your subconscious
trying to tell you
something.

Falling

Dreaming of falling (from a building, plane,
cliff, or something else) can mean that you
feel you are losing control of something in
your life. You might be feeling overwhelmed
at school or at home.

Failing a test

This dream might be the closest
to a real situation! You might
dream of missing or failing a test
if you're worried about an actual
test that's coming up, a project,
or some other challenge.

Being chased

If you are being chased in your dream,
it could mean that you are trying to run
away from a problem in real life.

Teeth falling out

Lots of people dream about their teeth falling out. If you have this dream, you could be worried about how you look. It could also mean that you're feeling nervous about a coming change.

Snakes

A snake in your dream could be fear showing itself. You might be afraid of something new or unknown in life.

Flying

In contrast to falling, flying dreams can mean that you are in control. You are feeling joyful and free. You're in charge and on top of the world!

Inspiration here!

Have you had any of these dreams? If your dreams are showing that you're worried about something, try to tackle whatever is causing that worry when you're awake. Talk to someone if you need to!

Number games

Test your skills with these number-crunching math games.

a If 2 is company and 3 is a crowd, what are 4 and 5?

b When Theo was 10 years old, his little sister was half his age. Theo is 25 now. How old is his sister?

Crack the code

Solve these problems to unlock the safe.

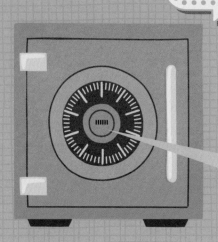

c A shopper spent $140 on a telescope and a bag. The bag cost $100 less than the telescope. How much did the telescope cost?

The code to open the safe is:

a [ ] **b** [ ][ ] **c** [ ][ ][ ]

Math magic

You can predict an answer with math that works every time.

Think of a number:
___

Add 4:
+ 4 = ___

Multiply by 4:
× 4 = ___

Subtract 8:
− 8 = ___

Divide by 4:
÷ 4 = ___

Take away the original number:
___ − ___ = ___

The answer is always 2!

Now try this trick on a friend!

Magic squares

Fill in the missing numbers in these squares. Each row and column should add up to the magic number for the square.

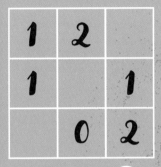

1	2	
1		1
	0	2

Magic number **6**

3		3
	4	
4		4

Magic number **10**

4	8	
9		1
	2	11

Magic number ⬤

How many?

Without counting, how much candy do you think is on these plates? Take a guess!

1

- - - - - - - - - - -

2

- - - - - - - - - - -

3

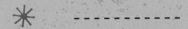

- - - - - - - - - -

Inspiration here!

'Math' began over 2,500 years ago with the Ancient Greeks.

59

Create the perfect playlist

Set the mood for any occasion with the perfect mix of tunes.

Occasion

When will you be listening to this playlist? Is it for a birthday party? If so, you probably want lots of upbeat tracks to get people moving. Or is it for study time? Then quieter songs might be just what you need.

Theme

Playlists work well if you have a theme holding them together. Think of the occasion and then find a theme to match. How about:

- favorites of the moment
- mellow listening
- show tunes
- all the feels
- dance beats
- soundtrack of your life

Flow

Music can affect feelings, mood, and energy. Think about the order of the songs in your playlist. Try gentle tunes to warm up, more energetic songs in the middle, and calming cool-down tracks to finish.

Mix it up

Remember that most apps let you play your songs in a shuffled order. So as much as you might plan your flow, be prepared for the element of surprise too!

Choose your tunes

Plan a playlist here. Choose an occasion and theme, then write down tracks that come to mind. Draw arrows or numbers to arrange the songs in the order you'd like them to play.

My occasion:

My theme:

What is your ideal vacation?

Take this quiz to discover the best place for you to recharge, relax, and have fun!

Start here

Which season do you prefer?

go out with friends

fall

On the weekend, you love to . . .

summer

keep your lips sealed

A friend tells you a secret. You . . .

spill!

stay home and relax

You go somewhere new. You . . .

explore!

gymnastics

rest inside

Choose an activity.

swimming

jeans and sweaters

In your wardrobe, you have mainly . . .

sunglasses and shorts

Adventure's calling

You never stop—adventure is waiting for you! You would love a vacation trekking through the jungle, exploring a bright new city, or snowboarding down the slopes. Go discover the world, brave adventurer!

Staycation

You are most relaxed at home. A quiet break by the fire with nothing to do but read, watch movies, or create is just what you need. Snuggle up and enjoy!

Tropical getaway!

You are looking for a true tropical vacation. You love to be free to soak in the warmth of the sun and dip your toes in the coolness of the sea. Dream of lying back and relaxing on the beach—just don't forget your sunscreen!

Star signs

Take a journey through the sky and discover your cosmic story based on the stars.

What is astrology?

Astrology is the study of the movement of stars, planets, and other celestial bodies and how they affect our universe, moods, and lives.

The zodiac

The zodiac is a flat map of the sky. It is divided into 12 sections, each based on a constellation found in that part of the sky thousands of years ago.

Aries
Mar 21 - Apr 19
impulsive, competitive, b

Taurus
Apr 20 - May 20
loyal, practical, reliable

Gemini
May 21 - June 20
curious, clever, playful

Cancer
June 21 - July 22
nurturing, sensitive, thoughtful

Leo
July 23 - Aug 22
outgoing, warm, ambitious

Virgo
Aug 23 - Sept 22
organized, logical, helpful

Pisces
Feb 19 - Mar 20
eative, sensitive, spiritual

Aquarius
Jan 20 - Feb 18
humanitarian,
revolutionary,
independent

Find your sign
Your star sign is determined by where the sun was in the sky on the day you were born. Some people believe it can tell you about your personality and how you relate to other people.

Capricorn
Dec 22 - Jan 19
ambitious,
responsible,
determined

Sagittarius
Nov 22 - Dec 21
adventurous,
energetic,
honest

Scorpio
Oct 23 - Nov 21
deep,
mysterious,
hardworking

⭐ My star story

My birthday: _____

My star sign: _____

Libra
Sept 23 - Oct 22
fair, agreeable, peaceful

Star sign compatibility

Use the chart to find out your fast friends, according to the stars.

What is star sign compatibility?

Astrologers believe that some star signs are well suited to each other. These signs are likely to connect on a cosmic level. They might have loads in common, or complement each other just perfectly.

What are your best friends' star signs? Do they match with you on the chart?

Your star sign!

Your friends' star signs!

Your star sign	Aries	Taurus	Gemini
♈ Aries Mar 21 –Apr 19			*
♉ Taurus Apr 20 - May 20			
♊ Gemini May 21 – Jun 20	*		
♋ Cancer Jun 21 - Jul 22		*	
♌ Leo Jul 23- Aug 22	*		*
♍ Virgo Aug 23 - Sept 22		*	
♎ Libra Sept 23 - Oct 22	*		*
♏ Scorpio Oct 23 - Nov 21		*	
♐ Sagittarius Nov 22 - Dec 21	*		*
♑ Capricorn Dec 22 - Jan 19		*	
♒ Aquarius Jan 20 - Feb 18	*		*
♓ Pisces Feb 19 - Mar 20		*	

How do I find my mystic matches?

Find your star sign down the left side of this chart. Read across to find your star sign compatibilities, marked on the grid by a star.

Inspiration here!

Some people have a "secret star sign." They might fall in one place on the zodiac, but they identify more with another sign. What do you think your secret star sign is? Does that change how you read this compatibility chart?

Cancer	Leo	Virgo	Libra	Scorpio	Sagittarius	Capricorn	Aquarius	Pisces
	★		★		★		★	
★		★		★		★		★
	★		★		★		★	
		★		★		★		★
			★		★		★	
★				★		★		★
	★				★		★	
★		★				★		★
	★		★				★	
★		★		★				★
	★		★		★			
★		★		★		★		

Grow a herb garden

Learn about herbs and grow your very own indoor plants.

You will need:
- ★ tin cans
- ★ thin card
- ★ felt-tip pens
- ★ potting soil
- ★ seed packets

1

Gather enough used tin cans for the number of herbs you'd like to plant. Carefully clean out each one. Leave to dry.

2

THYME   PARSLEY

Cut out a label for each can from your card. Write a herb name on each label, copying the names from the seed packets. Glue a different label on each can.

3

THYME

Fill each can with soil, to about 0.3 in. below the rim.

4

THYME

TIP
Follow the seed packet instructions for the best results.

Place a few herb seeds from each packet into the can with their label. Push the seeds down into the soil slightly with your finger.

5

THYME

Add water to each can. Don't overdo it —stop watering when the water doesn't soak in and sits on top of the soil.

6

THYME   MINT   PARSLEY

Place the cans in a sunny window. Continue to water them when needed.

Delicious decorations

Your herb garden is a lovely window adornment, but it can also be useful for seasoning your cooking. Take a leaf or two from a plant when it suits your dish. Be sure to wash the herbs before adding to food. Then chop or crumble the leaves as needed.

All about herbs

There are loads of herbs you might choose to grow in your garden. These are some common types.

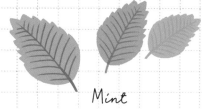

Mint

Refreshing mint suits both sweet and savory dishes. Add it to drinks, salads, and even desserts.

Basil

Basil is most famously combined with tomatoes. It is very versatile and works well in sandwiches, soups, salads, and sauces.

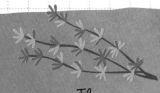

Thyme

Thyme pairs beautifully with other herbs such as oregano, rosemary, and parsley. Its leaves are so small that there is often no need to chop them.

Parsley

Parsley is a garnish that goes with nearly everything! It is mild enough to let other flavors come through. Use it to give a meat or veg dish some color.

Rosemary

Rosemary is flavorful but strong, so use it sparingly! Try it in dishes with garlic and oil, such as pizza or pasta sauce.

The art of calligraphy

Discover the art of this decorative handwriting and try creating gorgeous letters of your own.

Tools of the trade

To practise calligraphy properly, you might want to try:

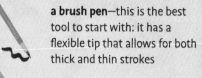

a brush pen—this is the best tool to start with: it has a flexible tip that allows for both thick and thin strokes

a dip pen—this is trickier to use: you need to hold it at just the right angle to work

From traditional to modern

Traditional calligraphy dates back many centuries. It had firm rules in the way letters were formed. Modern calligraphy is looser than traditional. People use it for writing letters, invitations, signs, and more. Have fun with it!

You'll also need:

★ a pencil

★ a ruler

★ felt-tip pens

The basics

Practice the strokes below over and over before moving on to letters.

Draw evenly spaced horizontal lines with your pencil and ruler. Letters sit on these lines, with their ascenders reaching the line above and descenders reaching the line below.

NOTE:
If you don't want to buy special pens, you could use felt-tip pens instead. Draw an outline of the thick and thin strokes, then fill them in to get a calligraphy look.

Strokes going down are thick. Use pressure with your pen.

Strokes going up are thin. Use a very light touch with the tip of your pen.

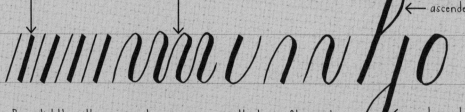

← ascender

← descender

Press lightly with your pencil so you can erase the lines afterwards.

Moving on

Once you feel comfortable with the basics, figure out your own style. You could curve the word instead of writing on a straight line, and add color with your felt-tip pens.

Aa Bb Cc Dd Ee Ff
Gg Hh Ii Jj Kk Ll Mm
Nn Oo Pp Qq Rr Ss Tt
Uu Vv Ww Xx Yy Zz

Practice makes perfect!

Practice strokes and letters here.

TIP
Hold your pen on an angle, rather than straight up.

Origami

Create delicate works of art using only paper.

What is origami?

Origami is the Japanese art of folding paper into cool shapes and creatures.

Fabulous fox

1

Start with a square piece of orange paper.

2

Fold diagonally up to the top left corner. Crease.

3
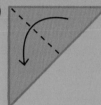
Fold the top right corner down to the bottom corner. Crease and unfold.

4
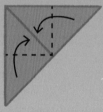
Fold the bottom and top corners in towards the central crease, as shown.

5
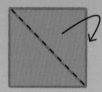
Fold along the diagonal, away from you.

6

Fold along the line shown. Crease and unfold so this section stands upright.

7

Press the middle section down outwards, as shown.

8

Press the top point down, as shown, to make a nose.

9
Fold the outer point in slightly, as shown, to make a tail to help your fox stand up on its own.

Enchanted forest

Use different sizes and colors of paper to create a whole forest full of foxes.

Bobbing boats

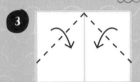

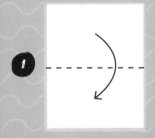 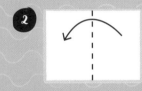

1 Start with a piece of A4 paper. Lay it vertically on your table. Fold the top half down to the bottom.

2 Fold the right half over to the left half, crease, then unfold.

3  Fold the two top corners down and towards the middle. Crease.

4 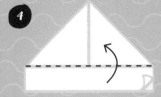 Fold the top layer of the bottom rectangle up over the triangles, then turn the paper over.

5 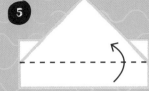 Fold the bottom rectangle up in the same way as step 4, then unfold it.

6 Fold each corner of the bottom rectangle in towards the crease, as shown. Refold the bottom rectangle up.

7 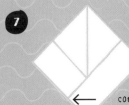 Tuck this corner under the flap below.

Pull the long edges at the bottom apart until the paper flattens the other way, making the shape above. Tuck in the corners as shown on both the front and back.

8 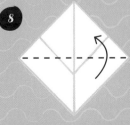 Fold the top layer of the bottom point up to the top. Turn over and repeat on the back.

9 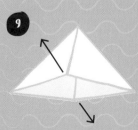 Pull the long edges apart and flatten the other way, as you did previously.

10 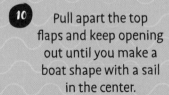 Pull apart the top flaps and keep opening out until you make a boat shape with a sail in the center.

Setting sail

Your little boat should float! Test it in a bathtub or sink. Then make more boats with your friends and race them.

Palmistry

Your future is in your hands...

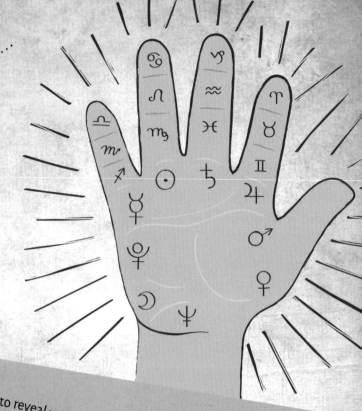

What is palmistry?

Palmistry is the art of reading your personality and predicting your future from the lines on your hands. The practice of palmistry is believed to have started in ancient India over 2,500 years ago. It is not a proven science, but it is now very popular worldwide.

Hand shapes

Study the shape of your hands to reveal your personality.

Earth

Earth hands have short fingers and square palms. People with Earth hands are said to be grounded, reliable, and practical.

Fire

Fire hands have short fingers and long palms. People with Fire hands can be confident, passionate, and driven.

Air

Air hands have long, spindly fingers and square palms. People with Air hands are normally smart, curious, and communicative.

Water

Water hands have both long fingers and long palms. People with Water hands are said to be intuitive, imaginative, and sensitive.

Palm lines

Now look closely at the lines on your hand to discover more.

Inspiration here!

Every palm and fingerprint is unique, so remember that everyone will have variations on these lines.

index finger

middle finger

ring finger

pinky finger

Head line

The head line relates to the mind and learning. If your head line is curved, you are likely spontaneous and creative in your thinking. A straight line means you are more traditional and practical.

Heart line

The heart line predicts your attitude to relationships. If your heart line starts below your middle finger, you are likely more focused on your goals. If the line starts below the index finger, you might be a romantic and good at making new friends.

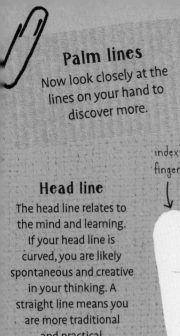

thumb

Fate line

A deep line means you are influenced by fate. If the line breaks and changes direction, you might be affected by other external forces. If your fate line joins up with your life line, you control your own destiny!

Life line

The life line is about your life journey and experiences. A long, deep line means you are full of energy. A short, deep line means you are good at overcoming problems. If the line is short and shallow, you might be easily influenced by other people along your journey.

Which hand?

There are different theories on which hand to analyze. Some people believe that the hand you don't use to write (your non-dominant hand) will show the personality you were born with, but your dominant hand (the one you use to write) shows how you behave in reality. Do you agree?

75

Splatter painting

Create an abstract art masterpiece, like those of the great Jackson Pollock.

You will need:

★ newspaper
★ an apron
★ a large piece of drawing paper or canvas
★ paint
★ paintbrushes

Jackson Pollock was an American painter famous for his messy paintings of splatters and splashes. He used a technique called action painting as he moved around and dripped paint on to a canvas on the floor.

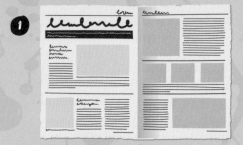

① Cover your workspace with newspaper. This art technique is best done on the grass outside. Put on your painting apron.

② Lay the drawing paper or canvas flat on the newspaper on the ground.

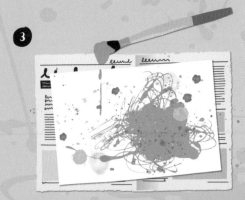

③ Dip a paintbrush in your paint, leaving a good glob on the tip. Use the paintbrush to drip and throw the paint at your canvas, making lines and shapes as you wish. Use different colors that represent the idea or feeling you are trying to convey.

④ Leave to dry, then hang your art!

Inspiration here!

"Abstract" means that the painting doesn't look like anything real. Instead, it is meant to represent an idea or emotion.

Salt art

Season your paintings with salt to give them a gorgeous new level of texture.

You will need:

★ watercolor paints
★ paintbrushes
★ painting paper
★ coarse salt

1 Paint a tree or nighttime scene on your paper with the watercolor paints and paintbrushes.

2 While the sheen of the paint is just beginning to disappear (but the paper is still wet), sprinkle salt over the painting. Watch as the texture around each grain of salt changes.

3 Let the painting dry completely. Then gently brush off any excess salt.

What's happening?

The salt absorbs the water around it, but it leaves the pigment (color) behind. This leaves lighter spots everywhere the salt landed. This technique takes some practice to get the timing and type of salt right, so keep trying and see what works for you!

Practice yoga

Follow this ancient practice to find flexibility, calm, and strength.

What is yoga?

Yoga is the Hindu practice of breath control, meditation, and specific body poses. It began as a way of religion and self-discipline, but it is now used all over the world for health and relaxation purposes.

Yoga poses

There are many forms of yoga practiced, at varying levels of difficulty. Try these basic poses to get started.

Easy pose

This common warm-up pose helps you slow down and focus on your breathing. Sit cross-legged with your hands on your knees, palms up. Close your eyes and count 10 deep breaths in and out.

Wear comfy, stretchy clothing so you can move easily while practicing yoga. Go barefoot to connect with the ground, or use a yoga mat.

Mountain pose

Mountain pose is the basis for many more difficult postures. It helps you find your connection with the ground. Stand with your feet together. Press down through your toes, draw in your tummy and chest, and gently bring your shoulder blades together. Imagine a string pulling the top of your head up towards the ceiling. Hold for eight deep breaths.

Remember to breathe

Breathing is a major part of yoga. Breathe in deeply through your nose, then exhale slowly through your mouth. Become aware of your breathing.

Tree pose

Work on your balance with this strong pose. Stand with your feet together. Slowly lift your left leg and place your left foot on your right inner thigh. Hold your hands in a prayer position. Find a spot in front of you to focus on to help keep your balance. Hold for six to eight breaths. Switch legs and repeat. Be sure to avoid leaning on the standing leg.

Downward-facing dog

This pose is an incredible stretch for the whole body. Start on all fours, your wrists under your shoulders and your knees under your hips. Tuck your toes under and lift your hips up and back toward your heels. Keep your legs as straight as possible. Walk your hands forward a little if needed. Hold for four breaths.

Child's pose

Complete your session with this calming stretch. Start on all fours, your wrists under your shoulders and your knees under your hips. Bring your butt backward to sit on your heels, keeping your hands where they are. Lower your forehead to the floor and feel your body release. Hold for 10 deep breaths, or as long as needed.

HEALTH NOTE:

If you plan to practice yoga often, consider joining a class. An instructor can help you be sure you are doing the movements and breathing correctly.

Mindful meditation

Find calm and boost happiness with these mindful meditation techniques.

What is it?

Mindfulness is all about slowing down and peacefully focusing on the present. Meditation helps you to do that.

Commit to calm

Meditation works best if it becomes a habit. Decide on a time of day, and try to meditate every day around this time. Find a peaceful spot in your room or home where you can sit undisturbed. You might even want to sit on the grass in the garden if the outdoors is somewhere you feel calm.

Inspiration here!

As well as bringing calm, meditation can help increase concentration, focus, and compassion in daily life. It might even help restless sleepers to fall asleep!

Techniques

Try these three techniques to get started. For each, begin by sitting on the floor. Close your eyes . . .

Body awareness

Bring body and mind together with this technique. With your eyes closed, focus on the very top of your head. Breathe in, then out. Move down to your shoulders. Breathe in, then out. Are your shoulders tense? Relaxed? Move to your chest and middle. Breathe in, then out. Be aware of how it feels deep in your belly. Finally, scan down your legs all the way to your feet. How do they feel? Are they uncomfortable? Relaxed? Let out a big breath as you land on your toes. Try this technique again, and see if you feel any different this time.

Finger release

If you're feeling tense or angry, this is a useful technique to help you calm down. Squeeze your hands into fists. Take a deep breath in. As you exhale, uncurl your left thumb. Breathe in again, and uncurl your left index finger as you exhale. Carry on slowly breathing in and out, uncurling one finger with each out-breath. After ten deep breaths, you should finish with your open palms resting on your lap. Enjoy this peace for as many more breaths as you need.

Remember to keep breathing as you work through this technique.

Mental sunshine

With your eyes closed, start by focusing on your body as it sits on the ground. Then, imagine a beam of light coming from the sun straight into you. Feel it brighten and lighten your mind. Then, imagine passing this beam of light on to someone else. Picture a friend or family member and see the light go from your body into theirs. This act of mental kindness opens your heart as well as your mind.

Coloring to calm

Coloring can be very calming, as you slow down and focus on the page. Try to relax while you color this pretty pattern.

Design a terrarium

Make a miniature landscape to bring greenery into your home.

What is a terrarium?

A terrarium is a small garden in an enclosed environment. These tabletop landscapes are perfect for adding life to indoor spaces, and make thoughtful gifts for a friend!

You will need:

★ a clear glass container
★ small stones
★ activated charcoal
★ potting soil
★ terrarium plants

Top terrarium tips

Try to upcycle or buy a used glass container. An old fishbowl, coffee pot, or vase would do nicely.

Find activated charcoal, potting soil, and terrarium plants at a garden center.

Choose a selection of plants that are small enough to fit in your container.

Leave empty space in the top third of your terrarium.

Water your terrarium regularly, as you see the soil drying out.

Place the terrarium in a bright spot, but not in direct sunlight.

Perfect plants

Terrarium plants need to stay small and thrive in humidity. Some good plants to choose are:

 mini ferns

moss

air plants

peperomia

Ask for help at the garden center, and carefully read the instructions on each plant's label for the best results.

1

Choose a container with a wide opening. You need to be able to reach in to set up your landscape.

6

Add a final layer of pebbles for decoration and to keep your plants in place.

2

Place a layer of stones at the base of your container. This creates a space for water drainage.

4

Use a thick layer of potting soil. It should be at least 2 in. deep for the plants to root into.

5

Make holes in the soil to place your plants into. Arrange them how you'd like. Have fun with the design!

3

Add a thin layer of activated charcoal. This fights off bacterial growth in the soil.

85

Word games

Play with your love of language with these word challenges.

ARDME _ _ _ _ _

RTAS _ _ _ _

SHIW _ _ _ _

TAERCE _ _ _ _ _ _

SOVCIDRE _ _ _ _ _ _ _ _

Scramble search

Unscramble these words.
Then find them in the word search.

A	G	W	I	S	O	L	E	A	F	S	E	A	H	R
S	E	D	U	N	V	I	L	W	I	S	H	E	A	T
K	I	L	I	F	O	A	H	S	E	R	L	T	C	A
A	D	R	W	S	A	I	C	R	E	A	I	O	R	I
D	R	E	A	H	C	A	R	I	S	A	T	E	E	B
O	E	R	I	M	F	O	A	F	U	T	A	R	A	I
A	A	L	H	O	R	E	V	A	R	I	A	A	T	R
R	M	C	A	D	R	E	N	E	B	A	N	R	E	T
A	G	O	R	I	A	S	U	N	R	I	S	C	O	S

Why did the foal get sent to his room?

He wouldn't stop HORSING around!

Rhyme time

Set a timer for one minute. Quick! How many words can you think of that rhyme with CAT? Write down as many as you can before the timer goes.

HINT:
Try to think of words with more than just one syllable too.

Challenge a friend!

Try this game again. Who can come up with the most rhymes with **BOY** in one minute?

Words in a word

How many words can you create from the letters in the word **INSPIRATION**?

Write them here.

star

Story builder

Play this game with a group of friends.

1 One person begins by starting a story with one sentence.

This game can be played by saying the sentences out loud, or you can write down your ideas to remember your wacky creations!

Why are fish so smart?

Because they live in SCHOOLS!

Where did your story end up? With all the different imaginations involved, the story might go in very crazy directions!

2 The next person adds one more sentence to the story.

Once upon a time there was a lonely unicorn.

This unicorn was afraid to fly.

3 The next person adds another sentence, and so on, until everyone has had at least one turn and the story is done.

But then the unicorn met a lonely dragon!

Host a slumber party

Invite your friends to a perfectly sleepy and special pajama party.

Party planning

Talk to your parents about when you can throw your slumber party and how many people you can invite. Decide where you'll have it too. Will friends sleep on the floor in your room, or will you take over the living room with all your beds?

The set-up

Ask each of your friends to bring a sleeping bag. Lay these out in a circle with your pillows in the center for the best chatting position. You could also lay out extra cushions and blankets for added comfort. For an extra magical event, drape blankets over the beds to make cozy dens.

Snacks

Choose a mix of treats to share with your friends. Try popcorn, chips, candy, and fruit!

Activities

You might spend a lot of the evening just chatting and giggling, but it's a good idea to plan some other activities to keep you busy. You could set up a scavenger hunt, play board games and cards, or even do some crafting or baking together.

Don't forget to have a plan for breakfast in the morning!

Candy

Start planning

Write down or sketch some of your slumber party ideas here.

Design an invitation

Turn your party into a proper event with an invitation to match. Design your own or copy this one.

You're invited to a

slumber party!

Day: ....

Time: ....

Place: ....

RSVP to: ....

Don't forget your pajamas!

Design a scavenger hunt

Inspire friends and family to notice the little things around them with this fun challenge.

What is a scavenger hunt?

A scavenger hunt gives a list of items for people or teams to find. The first person or team to find all the items is the winner!

What you'll need

Print enough copies of the list and pencils for each person or team who will be involved. Give everyone a bag to collect their items if they are meant to bring them back.

Some scavenger hunts involve collecting the actual items, while others simply ask for a tick or a photo. Decide on the requirements for your hunt, and make sure everyone knows the rules.

Pick a prize

Make sure you have an incentive that keeps people in the game. Choose a prize that your friends will love. It could be an object, such as a homemade trophy, or an extra-special honor, such as getting to choose the first song to play at a party.

Think theme

Think about where and when you'd like to hold the hunt. Will you be setting it up as a daytime boredom buster? A pajama party challenge? Match the theme to the occasion. Try these ideas, or dream up your own:

Road trip rummage

Tick when you spot a blue car, a driver wearing a hat, something starting with D...

Indoor scavenge

Find a green balloon, a fantasy book, something furry...

Nature forage

Bring back a stick, a helicopter seed, a red leaf...

Photo fun

Get a photo of something purple, a silly selfie, an awkward dance move...

TIP

You could set a time limit instead. The person or team to collect the most items in the time wins!

Design your own

Write down some other scavenger hunt themes and ideas here. Brainstorm items you could challenge your friends to find.

Your list might look something like this. Make sure everything on it is safe and allowed to be picked up.

Garden forage

a rock shaped like a heart

a pinecone

a long blade of grass

an acorn

three leaves of different shapes

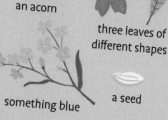

a stick shaped like a letter

something blue

a seed

something rough

Inspiration here!

Try designing a treasure hunt too! A treasure hunt gives players a series of clues that lead from one to the other, until they reach the prize at the end.

Make a time capsule

Capture memories in a capsule to rediscover and cherish in the future.

What is a time capsule?

A time capsule is a collection of items and notes that you put together now, to hide for your future self or family members.

Choose your container

Think about what you want to put inside and where you want to hide your capsule. Decorate a shoebox for indoor capsules, or find a more durable box if you're going to keep it outside. A clean jar or plastic tub works well too if it gives you the space you need.

Fill it!

There are endless options for things to put inside. Think about what's meaningful to you. What about:

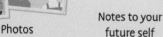

Letters

A magazine or newspaper to show current trends

Photos

Notes to your future self

A school project or award you're proud of

Favorite toys

A friendship bracelet

Hide it!

Once you're happy with your captured memories, close and seal the lid tightly. Find somewhere safe to hide your time capsule, such as at the back of a cupboard or buried in the yard. You could even ask a friend or adult to hide it for you so you aren't tempted to peek!

Aliya's time capsule 2020

Label your time capsule with your name and the date.

To me, from me

Fill in this page for ideas of notes about your current self that you might like to share with yourself in the future.

The most important thing to me is _____

When I grow up, I want to be _____

I hope that when I find this, I am _____

Advice for my future self: _____

My favorites right now:

Book: _____   Movie: _____

Color: _____   Activity: _____

Food: _____   Drink: _____

Dear Future Me,

....

....

....

....

....

....

....

Love, Past Me

.... (date)

Inspiration here!

Our bodies' cells replace themselves every seven to ten years. That means that if you wait a decade to dig out your time capsule, you could be a completely new person!

Learn Morse code

Send and share secret messages that only you and your friends understand.

What is Morse code?

Morse code is a system that uses a series of dots and dashes to spell out letters, numbers and punctuation. It can be sent by electrical pulses or flashes of light.

Giving a voice

The system was used for long-distance communication before telephones were invented. It was also used to send secret messages during wars.

Changing language

Morse code was invented by a group, including Samuel Morse, in the 1800s, to send messages by telegraph. Eventually, the simpler International Morse Code that we use today was agreed.

Hush-hush messages

Learn the code with your friends so you can send coded messages. Tap your fingers on a table to share secret thoughts or flash lights in the dark to get your message across.

Make a Morse code bracelet

Hold a special message close with a beaded bracelet threaded with code.

You will need:

★ embroidery thread
★ beads in three different colors

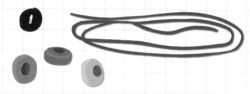

Choose one bead color for dots, another color for dashes, and a third color for spaces.

International Morse code

A dash lasts three times longer than a dot.

A •—
B —•••
C —•—•
D —••
E •
F ••—•
G ——•
H ••••
I ••
J •———

K —•—
L •—••
M ——
N —•
O ———
P •——•
Q ——•—
R •—•
S •••
T —

U ••—
V •••—
W •——
X —••—
Y —•——
Z ——••

Leave three units of space between each letter and seven units of space between words.

1 •————
2 ••———
3 •••——
4 ••••—
5 •••••
6 —••••
7 ——•••
8 ———••
9 ————•
0 —————

This bracelet makes a meaningful gift for a friend. You could spell out their name, a word that means something to you both or the word "friend" to tell them what they mean to you.

2 Fold a piece of embroidery thread in half. Tie a knot partway along the strings. Thread your beads all the way to the knot, spelling out a secret word in Morse code using the bead colors that match.

3 When you're done, tie another knot at the end of the beads, to hold them in place. Ask an adult to help you tie the ends of the bracelet together to fit around your wrist. Cut off any excess string.

Sketching techniques

Get out your pencil and add texture, shade, and interest to your drawings.

Hatching

Hatching uses parallel lines drawn closely together to add shading. The closer the lines, the darker the image looks.

Contour hatching

Contour hatching adds depth. Here you curve the hatched lines to create the illusion of a 3D object.

Sketching time!

Try hatching and contouring here. Use a loose hand to sketch freely. Remember this is a safe practice space.

  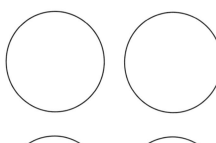

  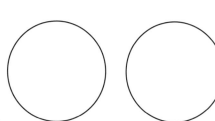

 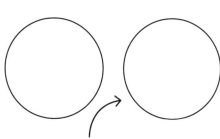

Can you make this box look extra-dark using hatching? Hint: you'll need lots of parallel lines very close together!

Try to turn this circle into a rounded sphere.

Cross-hatching

With cross-hatching, the parallel lines cross over at different angles to create even more depth. This technique can make an area look darker using fewer lines than with hatching, so it's a fairly quick method to use.

Shadows and light

Think about where the light is coming from on your drawing. Then shade in areas that would be in the shadows.

Practice on these shapes.

Don't do any shading where the light would hit the object directly. This creates an illusion of brightness.

Use curved lines to give objects shape.

Sketch the most crossed lines in the darkest areas.

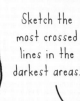

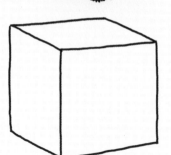

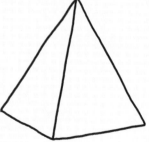

Inspired inventions

Inspiration can come from anywhere! Always keep your mind open to new discoveries.

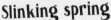

Slinking spring

The spring toy was invented by someone who was actually trying to create a spring to secure instruments on ships! In 1943, naval engineer Richard James knocked one of his springs off a shelf, and it just kept going, and going, and going. He and his wife turned it into a toy that has sold millions of versions across the world.

Crunchy chips

Legend has it that in 1853, in Chef George Crum's restaurant in Saratoga Springs, New York, a customer kept sending back his fried potatoes, saying they weren't crunchy enough. Eventually, Chef Crum became so fed up that he sliced the potatoes as thinly as humanly possible, fried them in grease and covered them with salt. 'Saratoga chips' were born and very quickly became popular further afield.

Explosive fireworks

About 2,000 years ago in China, a cook was experimenting with charcoal, sulfur, and saltpetre (all common kitchen items at the time). He found that the mixture burned. Then, when he put it in a bamboo tube, he discovered that it exploded! He experimented with combinations and colors, and fireworks were invented with a bang.

Sticky notes

In 1968, scientist Dr Spencer Silver was trying to invent a super-sticky sealant. Instead, he came up with a low-stick, reusable adhesive. Then, in 1974, Arthur Fry used this temporary adhesive to stick a bookmark into a hymn book. He realized he was on to something! The yellow color of the sticky notes we know today just happened to be the color of the paper available in the lab, next to where Silver and Fry were developing their idea.

What will you be?

Take this quiz to discover what you might be in the future.

Start here
Your friend is upset. You...

comfort them

make them laugh

No one is dancing at the party. You...

Your favorite books are...

start to dance and everyone follows

full of facts

chat with your friends

full of fantasy

You don't agree with something. You...

If you were an animal, you'd be...

protest for the cause

come up with another way

In a group project, you...

a dog

a cat

take control of the team

suggest ideas

A helper
You will help others to succeed—whether it's by treating patients, fighting for a cause, or supporting friends as you grow up together.

A leader
You will be calling the shots and leading and inspiring others. You might lead a company, a team or even the country!

A creator
You will change the world with your ideas. You might write a bestselling book, paint inspiring art, or invent life-saving medicine.

Look to the future

With inspiration behind you, the future is yours! What do you hope to find?

Looking back

Take a look at the last few months or the past year. Reflect on how you've changed and grown. You might surprise yourself!

I accomplished this goal: _____

_____

I reached it by doing: _____

_____

I tried these new things:

1 _____

2 _____

3 _____

I'm really proud of: _____

_____

I overcame my fear of: _____

_____

I was inspired by:

1 _____

2 _____

3 _____

Looking ahead

After reflecting on your past, what are your new goals for the future?
What can you do to make your hopes and dreams come true?

In the next year, I plan to _____

_____

I will do these things to make it happen:

1 _____

2 _____

3 _____

I hope the future for our planet is _____

_____

I hope the future for my friends is _____

_____

I dream that one day _____

_____

I pledge to inspire people to:

1 _____

2 _____

3 _____

Signed: _____ (your name)   Date: _____

Be inspired!

Are you feeling inspired to write a poem? Start a journal? Capture your dreams? Fill these pages with your thoughts and ideas.

This is a safe space just for you. Writing down your secrets and dreams might be scary, but it might just help them to come true too!

Be inspired!

Feel your words flow.

Be inspired!

Collect and write your favorite quotes in this space.

The time for adventure is now.

"Friendship is the only cement that will ever hold the world together."
– Woodrow Wilson

Be inspired!

Use these pages to doodle and sketch. Allow
your pen and imagination to run free!

Don't be afraid to try new things. Even marks you didn't intend can become something beautiful.

Be inspired!

Express yourself with art.

Answers

Pages 42–43

Riddle me this

What is so delicate that saying its name breaks it?
- **Silence**
What has a neck but no head?
- **A bottle**
I'm tall when I'm young and short when I'm old. What am I?
- **A candle**

What's missing?

Pages 58–59

Crack the code

a. **9** b. **20** c. **$120**
The code is **920120**

Magic Squares

1	2	3
1	4	1
4	0	2

3	4	3
3	4	3
4	2	4

4	8	4
9	6	1
3	2	11

Magic number
16

How many?

1. **19** 2. **37** 3. **65**

Page 86

Scramble search

DREAM
STAR
WISH
CREATE
DISCOVER

A	G	W	I	S	O	L	E	A	F	S	E	A	H	R
S	E	D	U	N	V	I	L	W	I	S	H	E	A	T
K	I	L	I	F	O	A	H	S	E	R	L	T	C	A
A	D	R	W	S	A	I	C	R	E	A	I	O	R	I
D	R	E	A	H	C	A	R	I	S	A	T	E	E	B
O	E	R	I	M	F	O	A	F	U	T	A	R	A	I
A	A	L	H	O	R	E	V	A	R	I	A	A	T	R
R	M	C	A	D	R	E	N	E	B	A	N	R	E	T
A	G	O	R	I	A	S	U	N	R	I	S	C	O	S